Spot the Diffe

Roots

Charlotte Guillain

Heinemann Library
Chicago, Illinois

Customer Service 888-454-2279
Visit our website at www.heinemannraintree.com

Designed by Joanna Hinton-Malivoire
Photo research by Erica Martin and Hannah Taylor
Printed and bound in the United States of America, North Mankato, MN
14 13 12
10 9 8 7 6 5 4 3

Library of Congress Cataloging-in-Publication Data
Guillain, Charlotte.
    Roots / Charlotte Guillain.
        p. cm. -- (Spot the difference)
    Includes index.
    ISBN-13: 978-1-4329-0942-0 (library binding-hardcover)
    ISBN-10: 1-4329-0942-8 (library binding-hardcover)
    ISBN-13: 978-1-4329-0949-9 (pbk.)
    ISBN-10: 1-4329-0949-5 (pbk.)
    1. Roots (Botany)--Juvenile literature. I. Title.
    QK644.G85 2008
    581.4'98--dc22
                                2007035759

Acknowledgements
The publishers would like to thank the following for permission to reproduce photographs: ©Alamy p.**13** (Wildscape); ©Duncan Smith pp.**12**, **23 top** (flowerphotos.com); ©FLPA pp.**15**, **17** (David Hoskin), **19** (Gary K Smith), **16** (Minden Pictures/MIKE PARRY), **6**, **18**, **22 right** (Nigel Cattlin); ©Grace Carlon p.**11** (flowerphotos.com); ©istockphoto.com pp.**4 bottom right** (Stan Rohrer), **4 top left** (CHEN PING-HUNG), **4 top right** (John Pitcher), **4 bottom left** (Vladimir Ivanov); ©Photolibrary pp. **9**, **22 left**, **8** (Mark Winwood), **10** (Bildhuset Ab / Scanpix), **21**, **23 bottom** (Botanica), **20** (John Swithinbank), **14** (Johner Bildbyra), **5** (Martin Page); ©Science photo Library p.**7** (DAVID NUNUK)

Cover photograph of a tree reproduced with permission of ©Photolibrary. Back cover photograph of black radish roots reproduced with permission of ©Photolibrary/Botanica.

Every effort has been made to contact copyright holders of any material reproduced in this book. Any omissions will be rectified in subsequent printings if notice is given to the publishers.
072012   006776RP

Contents

What Are Plants? 4

What Are Roots? 6

Different Roots 8

Amazing Roots 14

What Do Roots Do? 20

Spot the Difference! 22

Picture Glossary 23

Index 24

What Are Plants?

Plants are living things.
Plants live in many places.

Plants need air to grow.
Plants need water to grow.
Plants need sunlight to grow.

What Are Roots?

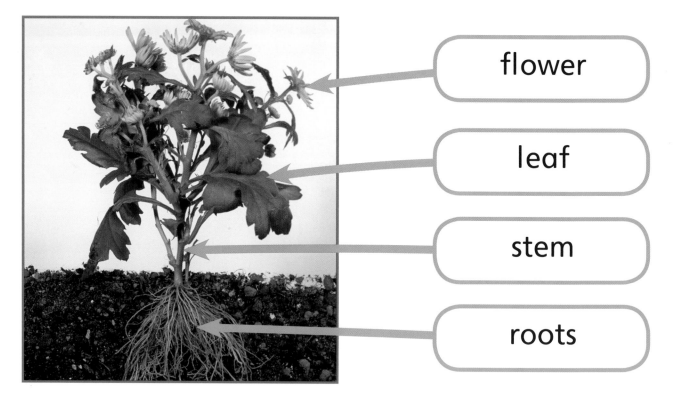

flower

leaf

stem

roots

Plants have many parts.

Most plants have roots.

Different Roots

This is a young plant.
Its roots are short.

This is an old plant.
Its roots are long.

This is a beech tree.
Its roots are thick.

roots

This is a leek plant.
Its roots are thin.

This is garlic.
Its roots are smooth.

This is ivy.
Its roots are hairy.

Amazing Roots

This is a water lily.
Its roots are in water.

This is an air plant.
Its roots are in the air.

This is a mangrove.
Its roots grow from bottom to top.

This is a banyan tree.
Its roots grow from top
to bottom.

These are carrots.
Their roots are orange.

root

These are beets.
Their roots are red.

What Do Roots Do?

Roots bring water to plants.

Roots hold plants in the ground.

Spot the Difference!

How many differences can you see?

Picture Glossary

smooth flat; does not have bumps

roots the part of a plant that holds it in the ground. Roots bring water to the plant.

Index

air, 5, 15

ground, 21

hairy, 13

long, 9

old, 9

plant, 4–7, 20–21

short, 8

smooth, 12, 23

thick, 10

thin, 11

water, 5, 14, 20

young, 8

Note to Parents and Teachers

Before reading

Show the children a plant with roots. Talk about where they would find the roots.

Can they think of a plant that would have very big roots? (Trees, bushes.) Can they think of a plant that might have small roots?

Show them a carrot and ask them to identify its root. Explain that we eat the roots of some plants.

After reading

• Go on a short nature walk and ask the children to point out any roots they see. Remind them that most plants have roots. Ask them to suggest which plants might have long roots and which might have small roots. Pull up a weed and talk to the children about the roots.

• Using a piece of paper, draw a line and explain to the children that it represents the top of the ground. Draw some different plants growing above the ground (tree, bush, flower, weeds, grass) and ask them to suggest what the roots would be like for each plant. Invite individual children to draw appropriate roots below each plant. Label the roots, (e.g., long roots, thick strong roots).

• Watch the roots of a sweet potato grow. Stick three toothpicks around the center of a sweet potato. Suspend the sweet potato in a jar, using the toothpicks to rest on the lip of the jar. Fill the jar halfway with water. Watch the roots sprout out of the sweet potato. Take a photo of each day's growth.